For Anne

DREAMS OF FLIGHT

With love from

Polly

DREAMS
OF
FLIGHT

POEMS

including six translations from German

BY

ANNE BOILEAU

ILLUSTRATIONS BY
BELINDA KING

ORPHEAN PRESS

2019

First published in 2019 by Orphean Press
10 Heath Close, Polstead Heath, Colchester CO6 5BE

Typeset in ten- on twelve-point ITC Golden Cockerel,
printed and bound in Great Britain by Peter Newble:
10 Heath Close, Polstead Heath, Colchester CO6 5BE
peter@newble.com ❖ http://www.newble.com/

ISBN 978-1-908198-20-4

British Library Cataloguing in Publication Data
A catalogue record for this book is
available from the British Library.

In memory of my mother,
Angela Boileau

CONTENTS

List of illustrations	page ix
Foreword	xi
Acknowledgements	xiii
Anne Boileau	xv
Belinda King	xv
The German poets	xvii

I. THE MEMORY OF BRONZE

The Visitation	3
Eve's Lament	5
Dreams of Flight	6
Ghazal: The Memory of Bronze	7
A Poet Showed me round his Violin	9
Too Fast too Swung	10
Epiphany	11
Trusting in our own Righteousness	12

II. THE WELL-TEMPERED PLANET

Autumn Day	15
The Well-Tempered Planet	16
My Soul in a Tangle	17
Hailstorm on Iona	18
Tarpaulin Cove with Jellyfish	19
Genetic Drift	21
Still as her own Reflection	22
Brother Anselm in the Herb Garden	23
Corncrake, Crake	24
In Iona Churchyard	25
Blue on Blue	26
Glorious Subterfuge	27
Earthworm Awakens	28
Relief	29
Open Letter from the River Colne	30
Let us Rejoice in Worms	31
Study to be Quiet	33
The Bindweed and the Thrip	34
J.F.K. to L.H.R.	35

III. STOCKHOLM TAR

A Black Day 39

Canal Bridge in Mist 40

Within its Time and Frame 42

Stockholm Tar 43

The Price of Sugar 44

IV. THE ARGUMENT

Declaration of War 47

Letter from Rye, September 9th, 1940 48

Snuffed Candles 49

I Had a Head for Heights 50

The Argument 51

Fallen Angel 53

Three Days in Grazalema 54

V. GIVE IT THE SHADOW

You speak too 57

Old Woman Writing 58

A Long and Fruitful Life 59

An Anaesthetist Spreads his Wings 60

A Circle of Remembering 61

The Tobacconist's Shop 62

Waving from Broom Knolls 65

Exhibits from a Museum in Sudbury 66

A Sort of Whip 67

A Post Script 68

Index of first lines 69

LIST OF ILLUSTRATIONS

Fool Tries to Catch a Lover's Dream   *front cover*
    Reduction linocut

Serenade   *page* 4
    Hand-coloured linocut

Kilpeck Musician   8
    Intaglio collograph

Three Women looking out to Sea   20
    Collograph and woodcut

Man and Beast   32
    Etching

Gold Seam III   46
    Collograph and screenprint

Kilpeck Angel   52
    Intaglio collograph

Flight from the Orchard   64
    Etching

Bread and Wine   68
    Intaglio collograph

FOREWORD
by Pauline Stainer

THIS lovely collection by poet and artist illumines the alchemy between word and image. Pen, brush, print, release energies in one another. These dreams of flight spill over many thresholds; lightweight, profound, delicate, passionate, even whimsical. Painter and writer exchange the eye of imagining. Landscape, seascape, the salt edge of things. Let the space between words speak magically into that deeper blue.

ACKNOWLEDGEMENTS

I WOULD like to thank the editors of the following publications in which some of these poems first appeared: ARTEMISpoetry, Across Frontiers (Camden Mews Translators, 2013), Ekfrasis Anthology (Mosaic Poetry, 2017) Freedom Poems (Poetry Wivenhoe, 2017), George Crabbe Poetry Competition anthologies (Suffolk Poetry Society), Shoal Moon (Grey Hen Press, 2014), So too have the doves gone (Jardine Press, 2014) Over the Water (Hearing Eye, 2007), The Link, Twelve Rivers and The Window.

'Study to be Quiet' won Second Prize in the George Crabbe Poetry Competition 2012. 'Snuffed Candles' won Third Prize in the George Crabbe Poetry Competition 2014. 'Hailstorm on Iona' won First Prize in Grey Hen Poetry Competition 2016. 'A Poet's Violin' won Second Prize in the George Crabbe Poetry Competition 2018.

I would like to thank Gregory Warren Wilson for his sensitive but firm criticism, Roselle Angwin for helping me find my own voice, Cameron Hawke Smith for help with the ordering of the poems, Pauline Stainer for her encouragement, Ruth Ingram and the Camden Mews Translators for our convivial and constructive workshops, and a great many fellow members of Suffolk Poetry Society and Mosaic Poetry Group. Without their true friendship and attentive ear these poems would never have been written and gathered together.

ANNE BOILEAU

ANNE BOILEAU

ANNE Boileau lives in Essex and has a strong affinity with its ancient landscape, its history and wildlife. She studied German in Munich and worked as a translator, interpreter and teacher. Her poems have appeared in various magazines and anthologies. *Shoal Moon*, a poetry pamphlet, was published by Grey Hen Press in 2014. Her translations of German poems have appeared in two anthologies: *Over the Water*, (Hearing Eye, 2007) and *Across Frontiers* (Camden Mews Translators, 2013). Her novel *Katharina Luther: Nun. Rebel. Wife* was published by Clink Street in 2016 and her accompanying audioplay, *Martin and Katharina*, has been performed to a live audience in Leipzig, Coggeshall and Halesworth. She is a member of Suffolk Poetry Society and Mosaic Poetry Group, Colchester.

BELINDA KING

BELINDA King studied painting at St Martin's School of Art in London. In 1980 she joined Gainsborough's House Print Workshop in Sudbury, Suffolk, for a while becoming chairwoman.

Many of her prints are allegorical, with sources ranging from mythology and religious imagery to dreams and memories of a childhood in Africa. The images do not stem from any particular belief, but rather from a search for our cultural origins and archetypes, which she uses to express feelings and ideas about the human psyche. She employs a variety of printmaking techniques, including screenprinting, collagraphs, etching and relief printing.

She has had many group and solo exhibitions of paintings and prints in the U.K., Germany and the U.S.A. Her prints are featured in *Printmaking, Traditional and Contemporary Techniques* by Ann d'Arcy Hughes and Hebe Vernon-Morris, first published in 2008, and *The Coach House in Gainsborough's Garden* by Miranda Mott.

www.belindakingartist.co.uk
Instagram: belindakingartist

THE GERMAN POETS

Brief biographies of the four German poets translated here by Anne Boileau

PAUL CELAN
1920–1970

THE son of German-speaking Jewish parents, Celan was born in Romania and grew up speaking several languages. He briefly studied medicine in Paris but returned home in 1938. The family were interned in a German labour camp in 1942 where both his mother and father died. After the war he settled in Paris and studied German philology. He married the graphic artist Gisèle de L'Estrange and they had two children, one of whom died in infancy. Always hypersensitive and psychologically fragile, he eventually took his own life by drowning in the Seine. He described his approach to poetry as 'wounded by reality and seeking reality'. He translated the work of many poets, including Rimbaud, Blok, Mandelstam and Shakespeare.

HANS MAGNUS ENZENSBERGER
born 1929

BORN in Nuremberg, Enzensberger was too young to go to war but was old enough to witness the devastation and brutality war brought upon his country and its people; he became aware very early on that his own country was in disgrace in the wider world. He travelled, learnt foreign languages and studied German and philosophy in Hamburg and Paris; he became a publisher and founded several magazines.

Like Bertolt Brecht, whose writing he admires, he highlights the tragedy of the human condition, while at the same time seeing the humour in it. He hates the dead hand of bureaucracy and all oppressive regimes and is grateful to have lived at a time and in a place when he is free to write what he wants and be published.

MASCHA KALEKO
1907–1975

KALEKO was born to Jewish parents in Schidlow, Galicia. Her mother was Austrian and her father Russian. Much of her childhood was spent fleeing persecution, so when the family finally settled in Berlin she felt safe and at home. She left school at sixteen but was soon recognised for her perceptive observations of 'the little people.' Her poems were published in magazines and news-papers and people loved them. At the *Romanische Café*, she met writers such as Bertolt Brecht, Hermann Hesse and Erich Kästner. In 1935 her writings were banned by the Nazis; however, she and her husband and their small child only left Germany in 1938, sailing to New York just in time. She had lost her mother tongue, and never gained much popularity or recognition in the United States, remaining homesick for Berlin for the rest of her life.

RAINER MARIA RILKE
1875–1926

RILKE was born in Prague into the German-speaking minority. He began his studies in Prague but then moved to Munich and became one of the outstanding poets of the twentieth century. Rilke's life was one of restless travelling. His writing was influenced by the periods spent in various countries and by his relationships with other artists. He was married briefly to the sculptress Clara Westhoff, and spent several years in Paris during which time he was secretary to the sculptor Rodin. He stayed in Duino Castle on the Dalmatian coast where he began to write the famous *Duino Elegies*.

He spent his last years at Muzot in the Rhone Valley in Switzerland. Rilke died of leukaemia at the age of fifty-one.

I

THE MEMORY OF BRONZE

THE VISITATION

by Hans Magnus Enzensberger

As I looked up from my blank sheet of paper
the angel was standing in the room.

A quite ordinary sort of angel,
presumably from the lower ranks.

You simply cannot imagine,
he said, how dispensable you are.

Just one of the fifteen thousand shades
of the colour blue, he said,

hold more significance in the world
than anything you might do, or leave behind,

and that's not even counting feldspar
or the large Magellanic Cloud.

Even the humble water plantain,
unremarkable though it is

would leave behind a noticeable gap.
Not you.

I saw it in his pale blue eyes, he was hoping
for a riposte, a prolonged wrangle.

I didn't move. I waited
until he disappeared. In silence.

SERENADE

EVE'S LAMENT

I DON'T know why you blame it all on me,
you know I only did it for your sake.
I ate that apple so we would be free.

Before you had to delve, my dearest, we
wandered in lush meadows, forests, lakes.
O Adam, please don't blame it all on me.

We slept in caves, caught clams in shallow seas.
Such plenty, all God's creatures could partake.
But Adam, you were longing to be free!

God said: *Do what you like; except that tree
is strictly out-of-bounds.* Yes. My mistake.
But Husband, must you blame it all on me?

I was beguiled; heard tell about a key
to end the nagging doubt. And then that snake
said, *Go on, Eve, just eat it. You'll be free!*

God cast us out. Exquisite misery.
We left the Garden. How our hearts did ache!
And ever since, he's blamed it all on me.
I ate that apple so we would be free.

DREAMS OF FLIGHT

EACH day at dawn over our house they fly.
A clamour of rooks from south-east to north-west.
Not far behind, a colony of seagulls test
more graceful wings against a salmon sky.
Walking with my dog by spikes of corn
I wonder where these birds might build their nests,
where peck and scavenge, squabble, take their rest?
Worms turned up by plough, seed freshly sown.
Our ancestors obeyed this route for long
before the Colne was channelled, marshes drained.
Men ran behind migrating aurochs, sheep,
and then by night they joined their kin in song;
crouched by crackling fires, told stories, yearned
to rise on wings like rooks; flew in their sleep.

GHAZAL:
THE MEMORY OF BRONZE

WITHIN its very substance dwells the memory of bronze.
Smiths at Giza treadling giant bellows forging bronze.

Two small pyramids back to back, the size of a cricket ball.
Hold it like a seashell, you'll hear craftsmen beating bronze.

Eight sides, eight faces: each displays a different attitude.
But every face and attitude tells the ancient tale of bronze.

It waits upon my windowsill, imbibes the heat of the sun,
Within its core remembering well the alchemy of bronze.

Take copper with a hint of tin or arsenic or zinc:
You have the stuff of resonance, church bells cast in bronze.

Before men thought to write things down, they extracted, analysed
And fired up fearsome forges, smelted ores, created bronze.

She weighs Gill's sculpture in her hand, senses gravity.
Anne has travelled to that Age when Man discovered Bronze.

This poem was written for the anthology Stone's Throw *(Mosaic, 2016),
a collaboration between local poets and artists paired up at random. My
partner was the sculptor Gill Southern, to whose bronze piece I responded.*

KILPECK MUSICIAN

A POET SHOWED ME
ROUND HIS VIOLIN

for Gregory Warren Wilson

A POET showed me round his violin.
He held it with a reverence all his own.
His teacher left it to him in her will.
The fingerboard is smoothest ebony.
A poet showed me round his violin.

Two types of wood, he said. The front is pine,
the back is spruce, from the Dolomites.
This maker always sought some minor flaw
in the grain he used. But it must not be weak.
Two types of wood, he said. The front is pine.

He does not spell it out, but it's implied:
we hear a breeze within, the breath of trees
felled on a mountain side under full moon;
the gale that broke the branch and caused the flaw.
He does not spell it out, but it's implied.

I wanted him to play but did not ask.
I had called on him to talk of poetry
and he prefers to keep to the task in hand.
He put the violin back into its case.
I wanted him to play but didn't ask.

But then he let me hold his precious bow.
Look at the mother-of-pearl, the band of gold
here at the base—but please don't touch the hair!
I felt the balance of it in my hand,
because he let me hold his precious bow.

A poet showed me round his violin.
Two types of wood, he said, the front is pine.
We didn't spell it out but it was implied,
I wanted him to play, but didn't ask.
Instead, he let me hold his precious bow.

TOO FAST
TOO SWUNG

BY the stream, rich goblets of gold.
I held a buttercup under your chin.
Then I lifted you up into the swing
that hangs from the snake-barked maple.

I pushed, you pumped, we had lift off,
leaving the ground behind until
the swing flew up too high, you cried
Enough, get down! Enough, get down!

I caught the ropes, plucked you off,
held you tight against my chest.
Thumping heart, open mouth,
silent until your lungs let rip

in a primal howl
then gasping, sobbed
Too much, too high,
too fast, too swung!

My hugging brought you back to earth
from that brief flight to the universe

and you were my daughter and I her mother
and I was my mother and you were me
and I was your granny and you were you
and her and me and they and we.

By the stream, rich goblets of gold.

EPIPHANY

for Sophie Campbell

TWO best friends are sharing a bath,
their bodies flat-chested, hairless, slim.
The tub stands firm on eagle's feet.
Brass taps, enamel studs: H and C.

It's Epiphany and so they sing
over and over and over again
a hymn about the Three Wise Men.
Brightest and Best of the Sons of the Morning.

It never occurs that instead they might sing
in praise of Daughters of the Morning.
Not a jot of rancour, their voices ring out,
echoing bright among tiles and pipes

as they wash each other's feet. Too soon
their bodies will grow hair in certain places,
breast buds will swell like little apples
and shame will veil their nakedness.

As they reach their prime, stomachs will swell
round as melons and they will give birth:
one to two sons, (brightest and best)
and one to two daughters (brightest and best).

And the earth will turn and time roll on;
bodies grow slack and slow, until
they hold in their arms the sons of their daughters,
the daughters of their sons.

But hold it there: this moment's enough;
they're ten years old, sharing a bath,
singing about Three Kings and a Star;
their hearts brim full of love.

TRUSTING
IN OUR OWN
RIGHTEOUSNESS

*'We are not worthy so much as to
gather up the crumbs underneath Thy
table, merciful Lord.'*
BOOK OF COMMON PRAYER

RAISED above their station
in the raking light of dawn.

As I wait by the kettle for our morning tea
I'm shocked out of an almost yawn
by slivers of moon-shaped Emmenthal
rich in gold translucency;

Each crumb entranced by its sense of self.

I shall not wipe the worktop clean.
Not yet.

Instead, I'll watch how every scrap
glows honey-gold in the low sunbeam;
how each crumb casts
its own excessive shadow
across the polished granite.

They're waiting to be gathered up
by me, who am not worthy.

Crumbs not underneath His table
but on the kitchen counter
for me
to marvel at.

II

THE WELL-TEMPERED PLANET

AUTUMN DAY

by Rainer Maria Rilke

LORD: it is time. The summer was so grand.
Lay your shadow across sundial faces,
unleash the winds onto the farmers' land.

Command last mellow fruits to drink their fill,
give them just two more southern, balmy days,
compelling them to their completion; chase
the last sweetness into the heavy wine.

Those still without a house won't build one now.
Those still alone, alone will have to stay,
will lie awake, read, write long letters, pray,
will walk in the avenues, up and down,
restless wandering, while leaves blow away.

THE
WELL-TEMPERED
PLANET

A HORSE'S leg is sprung to be strong.
A diatom is never wrong.
Look up, you'll see the sky is blue
and at your feet the speedwell too.

Barn owls fly with never a sound;
worms make soft the fertile ground.
Listen, be still, breathe out, breathe in
until you sense our planet's spin.

Our kind was made to resonate,
to watch, learn, imitate.
Horse, speedwell, owl and worm
know how it's done. Return, return.

MY SOUL IN A TANGLE

I'M holding a skein of heather-dyed wool,
   and my mother is winding it into balls.
      The dog's by the fire, the cat's on my knee.

Ben Hope veiled in a wimple of mist,
   Loch Hope sullen under purple sky,
      River Hope in spate, clear as tea.

The unravelling yarn tickles my hands,
   as she sings of Jura, Harris, Arran.
      She'll knit a jersey just for me.

The flash of a flank in a warrigal burn,
   the salmon are running, eager to spawn.
      Bewick swans on the wing, *free free free!*

A fiddler in Oban played me the song
   she sang long ago while casting on:
      You'll never see the Tangle of the Isles.

And now, on the early ferry to Mull,
   I watch the sun rising behind those isles.
      My soul in a tangle, mist in my eyes.

HAILSTORM
ON IONA

WHEN hailstones hit the machair
they turn into tiny shells.
When hailstones fall on rocks
they shimmer like oyster pearls.

When hailstones land on a scrap of wool
they capture the sky like crystal glass,
but when hailstones hit my open heart
I gasp at the pain, I gasp.

TARPAULIN COVE WITH JELLYFISH

Spirit that lurks each form within
Beckons to spirit of its kin.
RALPH WALDO EMERSON

TRANSLUCENT as full moon by day, a nothingness, the lowest form,
   more visible in its shadow on the ripple-sand sea bed
      than in its own substance
         in the sea.

Yet when tide pauses at the ebb and the surface broods as smooth as glass
   you'll see she bears a diadem of blue and turquoise neon lights
      pulsing like a heartbeat
         through her veins.

And when the glass-pearl planet turns to fold herself towards the night
   ten thousand phosphorescent lamps blink in a dance of resonance
      to all the constellations
         in the sky.

THREE WOMEN LOOKING OUT TO SEA

GENETIC DRIFT
for Elly

HER eyes were blue, the heaving tide,
she came to us from salty deeps.
Mearl and sea grass, krill and squid,
a flipper slapped down on the sea.

I see her father in the way
she crooks her finger, turns her gaze.
But laughing, it's my mother's laugh,
her sneeze my brother's sneeze.

A song, a look, a mood recalled,
a flipper slapped down on the waves. *
They turn and roll, break surface, blow
then curve back down into the deeps.

His forests of kelp, my bladderwrack
are twisty-tangled in this girl
who once lay swaddled on my breast
and suckled like a humpback's calf.

Mother and calf blow out—*whoosh!*
then curve back down below the waves.
I see my husband in the way
she crooks her finger, turns her gaze.

* *On their long migration north to Arctic feeding grounds, mother and baby humpback whales keep in touch by slapping the surface with their flippers.*

STILL AS HER
OWN REFLECTION

A HERON stands on a rock
on the edge of dawn
watching the stealthy tide slide in,
lapping, lifting bladderwrack.

Still as the rock, still as her own reflection,
she watches, waits for a fish.
On her mind, three hungry chicks,
a tangle of legs and beaks, in a tangled high-rise nest.

Was it her stillness that maddened the other?
Her rival the osprey flaps down towards her,
clutching like a briefcase a fresh blue-fish
that writhes and twists, scattering rainbows.

The raptor attempts to slap her head
with the tail of the fish, as if to say:
Look what I've caught!
But the heron ducks, avoiding the slap.

She could retaliate if so inclined:
peck out the eyes of two ugly chicks,
that wobble and whinge on a heap of sticks
on that post by Fisherman's Island,

but she ignores the taunt, keeps watch;
the tide slips in, smooth as glass. A flock of rooks
is flying east. Full moon translucent
in the brightening sky.

The flash of a flank! She strikes.
A silvery scup, gone in three gulps.
She launches from her rock,
fish squirming in her crop,

back to the heronry,
to three hungry chicks,
impatient for their mother
to regurgitate.

BROTHER ANSELM
IN THE
HERB GARDEN

ANSELM returns to his cell
After Prime, and bed. The bell
For Matins rings out, dispels
All sleep; he rises and tells
The Office, visits the Well
Sees the sun rise, hears the calls
Of birds piping on the Sound
And tends the ground, weeds the dill.

CORNCRAKE, CRAKE

CORNCRAKE, crake by the Abbey path,
hide your clutch in tufted grass.
Bluebells, summon wild bees to Mass,
Seahorses, break on the bay in the north.

Moored boats, remember to turn on the tide,
swallows, stoop where the burn flows clear.
Pilgrims, sit in the Chapel. Hear
Iona's silence, amplified.

IN IONA CHURCHYARD

KINGS asleep below the ground
may recall the tug of tide in the Sound
while we, alive, feel sun on our face,
hear the cries of lambs, sense this place
of ancient tombs. Random as the stones
that make up this wall, we've flesh on our bones,
a heart to beat, nostrils to smell
the salty breeze. Rosemary, speedwell.

BLUE ON BLUE

BLUE sky laid out upon the ground
around the roots
of hornbeam, ash and lime.

A nightingale in scrub willow
spills out
his rippling notes.

They bounce and drip
from sticky buds
between the sky and sky.

Suppose that I
should have no eye
to hear nor ear to see?

Nor nose to sense the thrum
of bells
and bumblebees?

Blue sky not just above the earth
but on the ground as well.
Absurd.

Or else? It is enough.
To stand at dusk
in Chalkney Wood
on the fourth of May

breathing
blue
on
blue.

GLORIOUS
SUBTERFUGE

BEN Fisher catches them at night
not with a rod and wicker creel
but in a box with a halogen light.

They hover and hunt in the cool night air,
exotic and varied as Cyclades,
in pastel shades common and rare.

A flake of lichen, scrap of bark,
a twig of birch or a withered leaf;
his catch sits quiet in the dark.

There's humour in their subterfuge:
We are not what we seem to be!
and cunning in their camouflage.

Ben holds a *Footman* in his palm,
a *Hebrew Character*'s on his sleeve.
Catchers of moths will do no harm;

a man who watches a *Poplar Hawk*
tremble and quiver on his knee
will never plot to start a war.

Flounced Rustic, Yellow Underwing,
Elephant, Spectacle, Buff Beauty.
Men of the cloth gave names to things.

Ben Fisher trawls for moths at night,
exotic as fish on a coral reef.
Captured but calm, they dream of flight.

Ben Fisher, amateur naturalist, discovered an unidentified moth in the
coastal marshes near his home in Essex. It has been officially named
after him: Fisher's Estuarine Moth, Gortyna borelii lunata.

EARTHWORM
AWAKENS

TIGHT as a knot.
Drought.
She slumbers
in her own clay pot.

Until raindrops
drumming soft
unlock
the confines
of her cell.

Recalling the joy
of friable soil
the smell of wet,
she loosens the knot,
uncurls.

Insinuates
her glistening point
up to the light,
the sparkling.

RELIEF

WHEN the lawn is yellow as our palest hen
and runner beans are drooping on their poles

the first delicious drops draw out a scent
which fills the air the senses and the soul

a blackbird opens his parched throat to sing
two pigeons fold their clattering wings and coo

drops bounce on lily pads and shining rings
expand link arms while damselflies flash blue

all worms all moles all trees can breathe again
as fired-pot earth drinks in the glorious rain.

OPEN LETTER FROM
THE RIVER COLNE

MY course was mine when I was wild.
I seeped and gurgled, oozed and flowed
through marsh, reedbeds, bogs and woods.
Amphibian cacophony; insects swarmed.
Ospreys swooped and bitterns boomed.
In flocks my wildfowl whirred and wheeled,
while otters grew fat on teeming fish.
Wildboar plunged, aurochs roared.

Then you arrived. You channelled me,
drained my land for beasts, for farms.
Boats with luxuries from Rome: glass, olives,
skins of wine. Barnack stone for Hedingham,
soft fleeces bagged and sent downstream.
Herons caught with lime, eels squirmed in traps,
your tables groaned with ample feast
of salmon, lampreys, clams.

You bathed your sheep and washed your woad,
you fulled your cloth and watered your crops.
Who drove those mills? Great plashing wheels
at Cannock, Bourne, Chalkney, Hull.
My alchemy turned grain to flour, fleece to tweed,
flax to thread; *my* power turned your wealth!
Come ebb come flow come high come low
I flowed, did not complain.

What now? Now what? No fulling nor milling
nor washing nor spilling? No laughing nor netting.
Forgotten? Spurned? Complacence, indifference;
but you need me still. I take your waste.
I draw it through my gravel and reeds,
send it out to sea . . . and out to sea . . .
another thing: (a secret, this): Watch me!

At dusk, or by night when moon is full,
or even by day (if you'll allow)
I'll bathe away your doubts and grief,
convey them down through Wivenhoe.
And still I flow towards to the sea
from Birdbrook through to Brightlingsea.
My course was mine when I was wild,
before you tamed and channelled me.

LET US REJOICE
IN WORMS

IN the beams of a very old house,
pea-sized heaps of sawdust
accumulate on picture frames.
Time is on their side.

In a cod's translucent flesh,
coral threads in layered pearl
flail in fear, confusion
at their host's morbidity.

Fine as string, whippy,
in a child's innocent stools;
fauna for a lively gut,
enhanced immunity.

In horse-muck rich as Marmite
spread at the feet of roses,
pink as petals of *Mutabilis*,
they munch, turn, cast.

Working waste in the compost heap,
reducing leaves at Assington Thicks.
Diligent in our tomb at the end.
Praise Him!

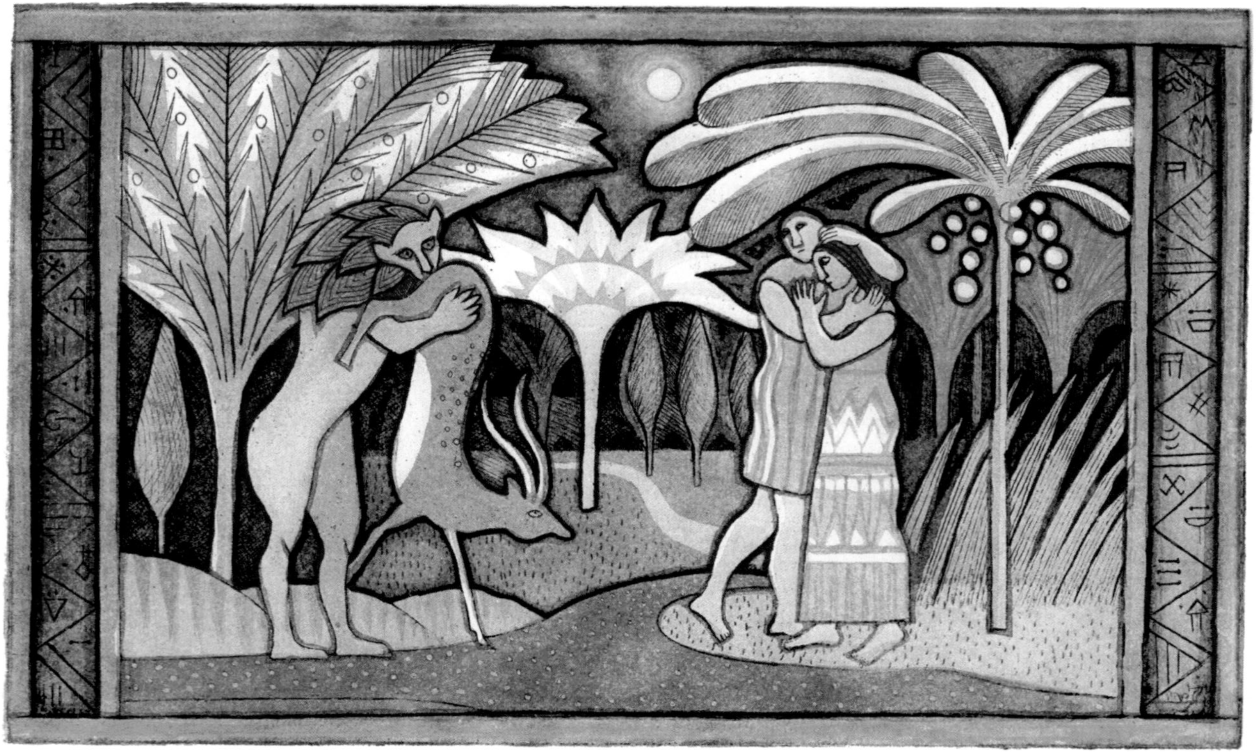

MAN AND BEAST

STUDY TO BE QUIET

HE sits under a willow tree
on the bank of a clear chalk stream.
In my coloured glass the river flows
through night and day and night.

At noon the sun casts pools of green,
of yellow, brown and blue—
they slide across the limestone flags
of Prior Silkstede's side chapel—
so mayflies dance, rushes nod,
warblers almost sing.

Darkness falls, the cathedral doors
are bolted fast. All is still. But when
the moon shines bright and full
my river is drawn up into the night.

Beside the Itchen, the Kennet, the Dove,
Izaak watches for the flash of a flank,
the flick of a tail, a slicing fin. His bait
grasshoppers, lobworms, frogs.

Men stand and stare at me, at him,
in hushed tones swap tall fishing tales
of flies tried out, fish caught, fish lost,
and eels. Ah, eels, now there's a thing!

At dusk he'll take his net, his creel,
walk back to his rooms to write it down:
the sermon which broke from its chrysalis
on a shaking reed as he sat and fished
and read and prayed beside the waters
which flowed, which flow, then as now,
of Kennet, Itchen, Derbyshire Dove.

Through dusk to dawn to noon to dusk
Izaak Walton studies to be quiet.

A stained glass window in Winchester Cathedral is dedicated to the author of
The Compleat Angler, *informally known as the 'patron saint of angling'.*

THE BINDWEED
AND THE THRIP

I ALIGHT on her lip. Should I venture inside?
Her trumpet's long, translucent, deep.
If I do go in then I can sleep
within her tube; it's bridal white

with a hint of pink, the flower smooth
as a new tuba; her throat is sweet;
when I sip her nectar; I'm replete.
Convolvula, I'm in love with you.

But does she even know I'm here?
Am I too small? I'm filled with doubt,
confused! O Bellbine, let me out!
Release me from my love, my fear.

J.F.K. TO L.H.R.

SWIFT as a dog-fish
she slices through the air
her right flank silver
from the setting moon.

Sleek as a mackerel,
determined as prayer,
her left flank pink
from the rising sun.

Pelagic fish descends
through her element, the air,
submits to Earth's pull
as her wings hang down.

Held safe inside her
the hopes and cares
of five hundred souls.
She's ready to spawn.

They'll open her vents,
letting in fresh air.
Viviparous cargo
released at dawn.

III

STOCKHOLM TAR

A BLACK DAY

by Hans Magnus Enzensberger

ON a Thursday such as this
even the most experienced butcher
can chop a finger off.
All trains are running late
because the suicidal
can no longer restrain themselves.
The central computer in the Pentagon
has been down for some time,
and all attempts at resuscitation
in the lidos have come too late.

And as if that were not enough,
next door at the Marotzkes,
the milk has boiled over,
the dog has trouble with its digestion,
and not even Aunt Olga,
the Indestructible,
is on tip-top form.

CANAL BRIDGE IN MIST

A STORY hangs about that bridge
like rags of freezing fog.

They say it was Epiphany 1853.

The congregation wait,
in best hats and coats.
Their breath forms clouds of vapour in the air.
Jack Frost has traced his patterns on stained glass.

The organist stops playing, the bellows rest.
Coughs and wheezes seem to be amplified.
Muttering ripples through the pews
It's not like him to be late.

Squire and Church Warden confer,
approach Miss Stranack at the back.
Perhaps they ask:
Was he quite well this morning?
We cannot hear what she replies.

A standing up, a shuffling, an emptying of pews.
The congregation trail out in twos and threes,
dispensing with the usual protocol,
and stand about in anxious groups among headstones,
gaze across the deer park to the frozen lake,
wrap shawls around their pale, coughing children.

The light is flat and monochrome.
Oak trees cloaked with hoar frost, twigs as thick as antlers.

They walk in file along the towpath, calling, looking out for signs,
but only one small boy scrambles down under the bridge
and no one stops to hear to what he wants to say.

They reach the Parsonage; Miss Stranack opens the door.
Oh no! She gasps. *His skates are gone!*
I caught him sharpening the blades last night.

They found him that evening at Osberton Lock,
half a mile down from Cascade Bridge.

Swift. Silent. Alone.
A young curate, and beautiful,
beloved of the people.
His first living would prove to be his last.

The sermon was still legible, folded in his pocket.
The Three Kings, of course. King Herod and his men.
And Rachel, weeping.

Ice is always thinner underneath a bridge.

WITHIN ITS TIME
AND FRAME

THE keeper struck the hare
behind the ears.
The kicking stopped.

He took his knife and slit one hock
then threaded the other leg through.
Here, he said, *take this to the van.*

I held its hanging heaviness
and cradled it. Round rib-cage, huge
under a soft, loose pelt.

My hands recall the springiness
of tufts between her toes;
dense fur cushions along her heels,

the sharpness of her claws.
A bead of red on her cleft lip,
a yellow stain under the scut.

In Dürer's painting of a hare,
she sits within her time and frame,
as tranquil as a pair of praying hands.

This hare sat in her form and watched
molehills erupting soft at dawn;
quaker grass bowed down with dew,
the breath of falling snow.

But the moon-fire in her eyes was gone
and what I felt with my small hands
and in my childish heart
I did not dare to say.

STOCKHOLM TAR

YOU push your heads through up-turned collars,
your throats constricted as we twist them
    round.

The traces coiled at your knees you stand
as girths are tightened, cruppers tucked under
    your docks.

We slip cold bits into your mouths, fix chains
beneath your chins, feed reins through rings along
    your backs.

Go back, we say, *go back*—obedient you
wait quiet between the shafts while breeching's
    fixed.

Should we assume by putting blinkers on
that we can stop you looking back at wheels
    and whip?

The driver climbs up, shakes the reins, you throw
your weight into the task; stiff leather creaks
    and wheels roll.

This is no servitude; we only need
to hear your tar-black hooves beat cheerful tune
    on metalled road.

You serve, but willingly. A fair exchange:
your sinews, size and vigour, for our decisiveness.
    That ancient pact.

The question's this: who's master and who's slave?
Great wars were never won nor empires built without
    that fierce love forged.

Stockholm Tar: *a kind of tar made from pinewood resin used to blacken
horses' hooves.*

Stockholm Syndrome: *Feelings of trust or affection felt in many cases of
kidnap or hostage-taking between the victim and the captor.*

THE PRICE OF SUGAR

ONCE it was cane. For that they lay,
manacled cargo in a foetid hold,
chivvied to dance on the deck each day.
They sang in rage, like blinded orioles.

Sweetness lifted from sodden ground.
Muddy beets tumble from the tilted cart,
thudding onto a rising mound.
Two tractors race against the dark,
'daws and rooks fly home to roost,
while a skein of geese is ravelling west.

In Newark refinery I stood and watched
men wade knee-deep in syrupy broth.
With shovels they scooped away brown scum.
Triangular trade. Sugar, rum.

IV

THE ARGUMENT

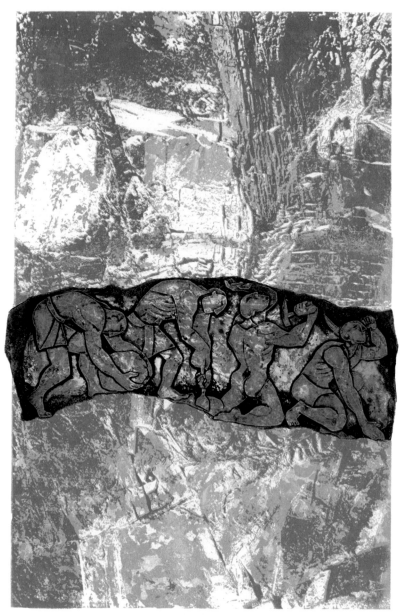

GOLD SEAM III

DECLARATION OF WAR

by Hans Magnus Enzensberger

IN the backroom of the beer cellar
where seven drunks are gathered
it starts, the war; it smoulders
in the creche; it is hatched
in the Academy of Science;
no, it thrives in a delivery room in Gori
or Braunau, on the internet,
in the mosque; the small mind
of the patriotic poet exudes it;
because someone's offended,
because someone's tasted blood,
in the name of God, war rages, on grounds
of skin colour, in the bunker, for a joke, or by mistake;
because sacrifices have to be made
for the salvation of Mankind, especially
at night, because of oilfields;
and that is why, because even self-mutilation
has its attraction, because money talks,
it starts, the war, in a delirium,
because of the lost football match;
no, surely not that, for God's sake; but then,
even though nobody wanted it; aha;
simply that, for fun, to be heroic;
and because we just couldn't think
of anything better to do.

LETTER FROM RYE,
SEPTEMBER 9TH, 1940

'extreme vigilance will be kept tonight as
enemy landing likely.'
WAR OFFICE INSTRUCTION

FROM the Martello Tower
I watched throughout the night.
 At dawn the sea was empty as
a conjurer's hat.

They do not seem to come.
And if they do, they'll meet our guns.

We're fighting for something.
I'm fighting for you.

Picture it: a fine domed roof,
marbled with dew; a lantern
throws strange shadows,
spiders creep about the wall.

I was on the beach, the sirens howled.
A hundred German bombers overhead;
one gun spoke, a second gun,
till twenty more
were plugging lead
with a music all their own.

One hit the sea with a fine white splash,
another hit the ground a mile away,
burst into a ball of flames.

If we get through this week,
the end is sure.

Today I saw two wild duck,
contented with their brood of two.

My darling, (may I call you that?)
write again soon.

SNUFFED CANDLES

I DREAMT the day-old chicks I had dispatched
came back to smother me.

It was not gas, I want to say,
but my voice was drowned out by their cheeps,
my airways stopped up with their down;
their cold feet scrabbled on my face,
they pecked my eyes and lips.

We snuffed them out in a large bell jar devoid of oxygen.
Three hours old or four or five,
depending on the batch.

How many lives did I dispatch?
Ten thousand in one week?
It was my job.

But do you know—and this is strange—
I welcomed them, those innocents,
the candles I had snuffed.

As I whimpered in my sleep
the cheeps the feet the bright black eyes
receded and

I'm sitting on a grassy knoll beside the river Dart
at dawn; and in the vessel of my palm sits one yellow chick,
much lighter than the egg from which he came.

One new-hatched chick or ten thousand,
disposed of by the very hand he sits in, quivering.
I believe he came for my redemption.

I awoke quite drained and weeping,
could not speak of it to anyone,
least of all my wife.

Five years ago I had this dream,
but only now can I bring myself
to write it down.

The male chicks, the yellow ones,
are surplus to requirements
in an egg-production plant.
It was my job.

I HAD A HEAD
FOR HEIGHTS

MY calves still ache from balancing
   precarious on rungs. But
      my head for heights is gone.

To look down now
   makes my head spin.
      I was a fireman once.

One mission finished it for me,
   I could never broach the smoke again.
      And yet, my burden was so small!

I smashed the window, clambered in,
   groped through smoke towards the cot,
      the drapes ablaze. Her pitiful cries.

I grabbed the crocheted shawl, tied
   the bundle to my chest and climbed
      backwards out into fresh air

and brought the child down. Her head
   like a herring on a spit,
      the soft hair gone.

Such heat, such smoke! The front bedroom
   beyond our reach, both parents lost.
      It was too much.

Light as a sugar-plum she was,
   and yet, when I remember her,
      she's heavy as a barrel of shot.

I'm done with it, stay on the ground,
   even when searchlights straf the sky
      and wailing sirens sound.

Just this:
   I saved a baby girl from fire,
      but lost my head for heights.

THE ARGUMENT

WITHOUT you I am lifeless tat,
a heap of rags, a dead fruit bat.
But give me the tension, the argument
of your downward tug, your feet on the ground
and the stubborn draught of a gusty wind:
I'll leap at the end of a twanging string,
strain at the leash, do crazy loops.

It's your give and take which lets me swoop
like the agile raptor whose name I snatched.
With your eye on me I'm safe, attached.
Just pull on my string and run. I'll fly,
an airborne dragon on a high.

KILPECK ANGEL

FALLEN ANGEL

FROM the limestone ridge
near Grazalema
a wide plain and a mountain range,
spread like a cloth of greens and golds
violet and lapis lazuli.

A griffon vulture glides
in circles up and up
around a thermal spire.

It plays its feathered wing tips
as we look down on the outstretched span
vast as Lucifer's.

His shadow brushes over us
and as he rises we almost smell
carrion on his breath, sense
the hunger in his frame.

He's gained the height,
sets his course,
slides down towards the plain.

By the main Granada road
a slaughterhouse for pigs.
The midden of offal glistens with flies.

Blood on faces,
blood on beaks,
they tread the heap with grace.
And feast.

THREE DAYS IN GRAZALEMA

THE day we walked beneath cork-oaks on the way to Grazalema
was the day before the day before the day you drifted on a dream
of pulling the cork on our vintage claret
    and pouring it away.

The day when Sally danced in the car-park at Grazalema,
when she turned into a swan at the age of sixty-three,
was the day before the day you shimmied into a dream
    of dancing away from me.

Sally showed us where red peonies grew blousy on the hill.
Those mountain crags above the plain! We gazed down far below,
watched a griffon vulture circling on fixed wings,
    rising by the cliff at Grazalema.

And you explained the principle: how gliders are lifted up,
lifted in a spiral on the thermals. That was the day,
the very day, you dreamt of stretching out your wings,
    and soaring off, away from Grazalema.

You and I could do it: we could drink and dance and rise on thermals!
But you didn't need to tell me how you longed be alone;
to drink, to dance, to fly solo,
    away from me, away from Grazalema.

V

GIVE IT THE SHADOW

YOU SPEAK TOO

by Paul Celan

YOU speak too,
be the last to speak,
have your say.

Speak—
Yet do not separate the No from the Yes.
Give what you say its proper meaning:
give it the shadow.

Give it enough shadow,
give it as much
as you know to be apportioned around you
between midnight and mid-day and midnight.

Look about you:
See how vivid it becomes all around—
In the presence of death! Vivid!
He speaks true, who speaks with shade.

However, the place where you stand is shrinking:
Whither now, you who have lost your shadow, whither?
Climb—feel your way upwards.
You'll grow thinner, less recognisable, finer!
Finer, a mere thread,
down which he wants to fall, the star:
right down, to swim down
where he sees himself shimmering: in the sea swell
of wandering words.

OLD WOMAN WRITING

for Kate Foley

WHAT was it about a postcard sent from Amsterdam?
What prescience drew her to that place?

The child imagines gabled roofs, canals.
Wide water meadows, pollarded willows
and stolid, sensible cows.
And sheep.

The old ewe never quite appeased
by the pelt of her own still-born
draped over another's lamb,
an orphaned lamb that was not hers.

Old Woman Reading—the light shines on
the Good Book but
it's the Gospel of her hands
that draws the eye.

And in the gospel of her hands
Kate held the waxy heads of newborn lambs.

This *Sage femme* knew the taste of disappointment,
turned the gall of her own pain around,
and ground it into a healing paste
to assuage pain in others.

And then of course those towering elms;
they once held up the Suffolk skies
but now are gone. She loved them too.
They still reside in Amsterdam, dispensing
pale green snow in spring,
blocking gutters, flowering canals.

This *Old Woman Writing* who we celebrate,
her face, like Rembrandt's, lined, lived in.
Wanting roots, she searches in the soil
for evidence of lives lived long ago,
stories of skill, endeavour, loss and love.

Who fashioned her own loss into the art
of looking and of finding. Found in Amsterdam
a woman who only had to smile
to light up a whole room; Tonnie
turned her smile on Kate, became her wife.

A LONG AND
FRUITFUL LIFE

*for Dorothea Boggis Rolfe on her
100th birthday. 17th January 2015*

YOU'VE put down roots in Wormingford
just like the trees around your house.

When someone calls, you give them fruit;
mulberries, gooseberries, currants, figs.
Or, if it's winter, a pot of jam.

Year on year,
you've gathered sweetness into jars,
for other people to enjoy.

You never learnt to drive a car,
had no need to be somewhere else.
And yet it was a faulty clutch
that brought a young man to the door
of your parents' house in Henley.

Love at first sight.
You were sixteen.
So like an owl in silent flight
you set out in pursuit of him.

You applied for work at his parents' farm,
milked the cows at dusk, at dawn,
to be on hand for news of him.
The war.

The man you loved was home on leave.
You were bottling pears in the scullery;
Oh, that's where you are!
He took a bite out of a comice,
put it down and took your hand.
Will you marry me?

You were together for sixty years,
yet even now the smell of pears
evokes that memory.

AN ANAESTHETIST
SPREADS HIS WINGS

for Ronnie Green on his 95th
birthday. 3rd January 2015

FOR forty years you refined the art
of inducing sleep. But in your heart
lay dormant a love of insects in flight,
of dragonflies, moths; the rustle at night
of creatures that creep and forage through leaves
and the twisted roots of ancient trees.
Of meadows where owls on silent wings
glide pale as ghosts. Where warblers sing.

You retired with Molly to a watermill
on the river Colne; you bought a field
to protect the hedgerows, sow wild flowers,
so children might spend innocent hours
chasing through grass, attending to moths,
observing the warp and weft of the cloth
of our woven planet. You created a wood,
named it for Molly. And Lo—It was good!

A CIRCLE OF REMEMBERING

in memoriam *Stessa Wood*

A DERELICT barn, barbed wire ragged
with scraps of wool. Abandoned pigsties.
Can this be right? Then a carved oak sign:
CAR PARK. Other cars nose up the track,
hesitate, park.

Strangers in sombre clothes climb out.
Is this the place? We walk in silence up the hill
past gnarled oaks in full foliage.
Flax and harebells mirror the sky,
calling to mind her eyes.

A recent plantation of native trees,
each with a modest sign:
Name. Dates. Nothing more.
And now, a fresh hole in the ground,
draped with green baize cloth.

The hearse arrives; four men in black
slide a wicker casket from the tailgate.
They hoist it up, link arms, bear
her coffin to the appointed place;
set it down beside the grave; withdraw.

As we stand in an awkward circle,
a miracle!
Out of nowhere, from a clear blue sky,
a pattering on jackets; a coolness on skin,
a sudden, glorious fragrance.

The first rainfall in eleven weeks.
Birds explode in song.
The hard-baked ground
exhales its joy. Umbrellas snap open
one by one, a circle of remembering.

She had a net, caught butterflies,
soothed them in a chloroform jar,
pinned them to a specimen board.
Next day she bade them fly afresh
in vibrant poster paints.

I think she must have sent that rain.
My long lost-friend, so briefly found,
then lost, then lost again.

THE TOBACCONIST'S SHOP

I

A TOBACCONIST'S Shop after closing time. No one.
In glass fronted cabinets single cigarettes
lie in rows, some with shiny golden bands;
boxes of cigars, packs of cigarettes.
From the ceiling, copper bowls hang
motionless on chains.
Earthenware jars stand side by side,
out of reach on a high shelf.

Behind the counter, curvaceous pipes
of cherry, rosewood, meerschaum
lie in voluptuous satin-lined cases.
Prices are concealed.

In the bay window on three glass shelves,
A row of labelled, coloured jars.
Here is a temple to a discredited faith.
The Litany not yet quite forgotten:
Dunhill, Smooth Virginia, Players Navy Cut, Capstan Navy Cut.

II

The rich autumn aroma inside the shop
brings back to me those men I've known
who used to smoke. I say used to,
not because they've given it up
but because they've died.

My father with his pipe, his pouch, his multi-coloured pipe cleaners.
He showed me how to twist them into horses and giraffes.

Uncle Hubert with his Havana cigars,
and a silver device to clip and trim the ends.
The smell of that smoke stings my throat.

Cousin Ralph with his pipe;
whose prequel to any meaningful conversation
must be endured by the visitor:
scrape it, shake it, re-assemble with stem,
fill with moist, layered tobacco,
tamp it down with the yellowed index finger;
take out the lighter, click up a flame; allow that flame
to be drawn in; the bubbly sound of suck.
Now he can relax, enjoy the inhalation.
Now he turns his gaze on me.
Now we may talk.

III

Where has it gone, that ritual between men?
The once indispensable quadrille of courtesy?
A silver cigarette-case, opened like a prayer book;
the proffering, the acquiescence; the *tap tap tap* (no filters then).

One takes out an embossed, initialed lighter;
it fits in his hand like a shell; and with a restrained and practised flourish
presents a flame to the other's cigarette,
lights his own from that same flame,
returns the lighter to his waistcoat pocket.

IV

Little affection resides between these two;
one may resent the other because he's courting his daughter;
or has been offered preferment over him;
or is paying more than decent attention to his wife;
or draws a larger salary than he deserves;
or has pretensions above his station.

But: we can be civilized, you and I.
Let us conceal in fragrant smoke
whatever frustration or anger or fear or contempt
might be simmering.
This is the dance, the ritual.

V

I think of those men I knew and loved,
savouring their cigarettes, pipes, cigars;
and don't forget those less reputable men
—I loved them too—
who rolled their own with who knows what
dubious substances?

And I hope that they might all be up there,
gathered around a crystal table,
ministered to by angels, teased by cherubs,
serenaded by seraphim.

They are easy, convivial, mellow.
They are blowing holy smoke rings into the clouds,
their differences forgotten,
united by the ritual and paraphernalia of tobacco.

They are at rest. Their lungs pristine.
An autumn aroma of leathery leaves
fills the celestial air.
Bless them.

FLIGHT FROM THE ORCHARD

WAVING FROM
BROOM KNOLLS

for Rosemary Morris

SHE saw things with a keenness all her own,
inspired a play about a foal that danced,*
and tended wounded birds who'd been shot down.

She found her Father's diaries from World War One,
set pages up with his photos, battle plans,
fine-tuning with a keenness all her own.

She watched out for her friends who lived alone,
encouraged them to take another chance,
cherishing wounded birds who'd been shot down.

Lambs and bullocks flourished at Pattinson's,
but she grieved to watch them loaded on the van,
suffering with a keenness all her own.

Her steak and kidney pud? Second to none;
comfort food for friends too thin or wan,
she fattened up her birds who'd been shot down.

I made mistakes; she did not condone,
but never judged; instead, asked me to dance!
She understood with a keenness all her own.

Dawn chorus in Lawford Church.† We file in.
She's waving to the train from Broom Knolls Hill,
while her grounded birds ascend on healed wings.
She sees things with a keenness all her own.

---

* *Tom Morris, Rosemary's son, directed* War Horse *at the National Theatre; she had suggested Michael Morpurgo's book could be adapted for the stage, and the foal inspired the puppet.*

† *Jenny Francis, Rosemary's sister, made a recording of the dawn chorus at Humberlands and it was played and embellished with a composition by Rosemary's grandson, Charlie Morris.*

EXHIBIT FROM A MUSEUM IN SUDBURY

HE kept me in his pocket on a silver chain,
scooped me out, consulted me.
His keen eyes followed my shifting hands,
returned my steady gaze.

I ticked to the rhythm of his beating heart,
moved with the rise and fall of his breath.
I shook to his laughter,
lay quiet with his doubt.

My mainspring thrummed with horsehair on gut
as he sawed his fiddle with musical friends.
The smell of linseed, the shush of his brush
as it dipped and touched, dipped and stroked.

Punctilious, he wound me every night.
But they've lost the key. I lie inert
in a showcase at my Owner's house,
unchained, unwound, no hands, no use.

Unable to run, unable to die,
an obsolete precision machine.
Time can stop and Time can fly.
Mortality. What does it mean?

Inside my case his name's inscribed,
Thomas Gainsborough. I have my pride!
I lodged with a painter in his prime.
He treasured me. I measured time.

A SORT OF WHIP

for Angela Boileau

WHEN I'm no longer here, those charged
with clearing out my worldly goods
won't know the knobbled rosewood stick
with silver band and leather base
propped in the garage by the rabbit hutch
was once Great-Grandma's driving whip.

Nor will they know, still less recall,
the day we drove the governess cart
from Elkesley Moor to Osberton.
We met a hanging holly branch, lowered our heads,
but not the whip. It snapped. Oh dear!
Its tapered thong trailed down.

That night by the Rayburn my mother
took the broken thing, tried out
how the severed lengths might fit.
A tube of glue, some fishing line,
I held it for her as she bound it round
and round with waxed silk thread.

How deft she was!
A thousand meditative hours, plaiting manes,
tying flies, knitting woollies, sharpening quills. Yes, quills!
One thumb was slightly bent, deformed—
a long-ago race with cousin Hans—
rolling down Hod Hill.

She could juggle with five eggs or was it four?
Sang silly songs while whistling.
Her *pease pudding hot* went unchallenged.
One day, though, she tied her final fishing fly,
put away her knitting bag, trimmed
the last goose-feather quill.

What's this? They'll say. *Some sort of whip.*
Broken, though.
In the fire or on the skip?

67

A POST SCRIPT

by Mascha Kaleko

A LETTER arrived from my old solicitor. He writes as ever,
factual, technical. Your obedient servant.

I almost overlooked
the Post Script.

'Now, as the evening of my life draws in
and that dark angel's wingbeats are beginning,
on some nights, to drown out the beating of my heart,
I want, dear Madam, to tell you just one time:
I have loved you for thirty years.

Now an ocean lies between me and you.
And I always wait in the hope that one more letter,
not a love letter, but, yes, a butterfly
might flutter across the heaps
of files and briefs into my life.'

BREAD AND WINE

INDEX OF FIRST LINES

A derelict barn, barbed wire ragged ... ... *page* 61
A heron stands on a rock 22
A horse's leg is sprung to be strong 16
A letter arrived from my old solicitor. He writes as ever 68
A poet showed me round his violin 9
A story hangs about that bridge 40
A Tobacconist's Shop after closing time. No one 62
Anselm returns to his cell 23
As I looked up from my blank sheet of paper 3
Ben Fisher catches them at night 27
Blue sky laid out upon the ground 26
By the stream, rich goblets of gold 10
Corncrake, crake by the Abbey path 24
Each day at dawn over our house they fly 6
For forty years you refined the art 60
From the limestone ridge 53
From the Martello Tower 48
He kept me in his pocket on a silver chain 66
He sits under a willow tree 33
Her eyes were blue, the heaving tide 21
I alight on her lip. Should I venture inside? 34
I don't know why you blame it all on me 5
I dreamt the day-old chicks I had dispatched 49
I'm holding a skein of heather-dyed wool 17
In the backroom of the beer cellar 47
In the beams of a very old house 31
Kings asleep below the ground 25
Lord: it is time. The summer was so grand 15
My calves still ache from balancing 50
My course was mine when I was wild 30
On a Thursday such as this 39
Once it was cane. For that they lay 44
Raised above their station 12
She saw things with a keenness all her own 65
Swift as a dog-fish 35
The day we walked beneath cork-oaks on the way to Grazalema ... 54
The keeper struck the hare 42
Tight as a knot 28
Translucent as full moon by day, a nothingness, the lowest form ... 19
Two best friends are sharing a bath 11
What was it about a postcard sent from Amsterdam? 58
When hailstones hit the machair 18
When I'm no longer here, those charged 67
When the lawn is yellow as our palest hen 29
Within its very substance dwells the memory of bronze 7
Without you I am lifeless tat 51
You push your heads through up-turned collars 43
You speak too 57
You've put down roots in Wormingford 59